the secret place

William Simon

Where can I go
To get away?

I just need
Somewhere to pray.

the secret place

the secret place

Don't be scared of God,
But instead, fear hurting God.

There is no fear
In perfect love,
And isn't Christ perfect?

The new covenant
Doesn't call for fear,
It calls for love.

And loving someone
Means not causing them harm.

How can you love God
If you don't fear hurting

Him.

Imago Dei

The Image of God,
You were created.

So why look downcast
On your outside appearance?

Isn't it the inside
By which Jesus sees you?

Did he judge the lepers
By their skin
Or their faith?

And to what are
You comparing yourself?

How can you say
One of God's images
Is beautiful,
But another isn't?

When you feel
The need to compare,
You need to declare,
There is no win
In comparison.

the secret place

"I don't go to church
They hurt me too much."

But is this statement a crutch?

I encourage you
To look at the one you follow
And the one that filled your hollow.

Jesus attended synagogue
And stood among His peers,
Who would cause His mother's tears.

The church is sometimes dark,
And no one can deny that.

But let your light be a spark
To ignite the flame
That glorifies

His name.

"Here are the instructions,
Now build my church"
Says Jesus.

We are given
Clear instructions,
But sometimes it looks
Like a piece is missing.

People claim to be Christian,
Yet act the opposite.

Were the instructions unclear?
Or were the pieces
Assembled wrong?

Did we put more
Emphasis on rules
Rather than loving
One another?

Rules didn't change hearts,
Rules didn't change lives.

But instead,
Radical love did.

the secret place 5

"Jesus that perfume
Cost her a year's wage,"
Says Judas.

I admire her sacrifice,
And what a great one it is,
But money isn't everything.

If only you realized
How much more
Life is than materials.

Soon, your wants
Will be your downfall,
But it will be too late.

Your bones lie in the dust,
And the riches with it.

My miracles were never enough
For your empty heart,
Satisfaction never came,
But a betrayal did.

The silver was never worth
What was given in return.

Less is more,
And the wooden cross remains
Greater than those silver coins,
Says Jesus.

Don't you live
Within me?

Why does it feel
Like sin owns me.

You died for me
To come close,
But It seems like
All I do is run away.

But just as the prodigal,
I will return,

And the underserving feast

Is served.

"You shouldn't be here
I'm a Samaritan,"
She exclaims.

"You're right,
That's why I'm here,"
Says Jesus.

If the unknown
Are never searched for,
How can they know
That they are lost?

Jesus was a carpenter,
And was around tools often.

Did He ever see the nail
That would be driven
Into His body?

Did He ever get a splinter
And wonder how it would
Feel to have thorns in His skull?

I know He knew the pain.
He tried to pray for
Another way.

But His love remained.

"I did it again
I'm not worthy."

"You're right,
You never were,"
Says Jesus.

That's why I'm here
When you fall,
But you have to get up.

I can't be a crutch
Without the intent
Of you wanting to be

Healed.

Im nothing special,
So why me?

I go against you,
I try my own way.

So why me?

If *my love* were limited,
Only to the deserving,
Then who would experience it?

A tree starts small,
But that sapling
Will soon grow tall.

The trees branches
Will grow wide,
And the leaves
Will multiply.

The more it grows,
The more responsibility it owns.

If trouble invades,
Is it any less a tree?

The church is a large vessel,
Growing and expanding,
With more people representing.

Presenting more opportunity for mistake,
Bad actors will come,
Weakening the church.

But a dead branch
Doesn't weaken *the roots.*

The church remains.

"I read my Bible every day!"
We tell Jesus.

"The church
Wasn't built on the Bible;
It was built on the cross."

"I'm telling them
About you, Jesus."

"A sign about Hell
Isn't telling them
About *my* love."

How can you condemn
Someone for something
They don't follow?

Forced follow by fear
Doesn't grow the church;
It destroys it.

My message wasn't force;
It was grace by faith, in choice.

If my free grace
Is sufficient for you,
Why can't it be for them?

the secret place

If my kingdom was about force,
Wouldn't I have already taken it?

So, why is this your approach?

I walked the earth
And chose to die to it,
Despite having the power
To conquer it.

Your picket sign of Hell
Doesn't scare anyone,
When you have convinced
Them to accept it.

I wasn't hated for hating,
I was hated for loving those
In which I wasn't supposed to.

Hurt people, hurt people.

But why do People who claim
To be Christ followers
Hurt people?

"Jesus will make you happy!"
As they yell at you with a sign
"You're going to Hell."

Jesus never hurt,
So why do His followers?

I'm not sure,
I can't explain it.

They lecture about the law,
But don't follow it themselves.

The changed heart
Follows the law.
It's evidence of the Spirit.

But one must
Have the Spirit
To change.

The law matters
Only after a belief
Turns into a

Lifestyle.

the secret place

A tree started the fall,
And a tree ended the fall.

Two different outcomes,
Yet it all comes back to
The tree.

You can always be used.

Will it be
For sin or servitude?

You must decide
What's more important.

This life for you,
Or the seed you plant
In someone else's life.

A seed left behind
Could produce a cross
That changes the world.

"Wipe your feet at the door
And don't come in till they're clean,"
Says the world.

"No need to wipe your feet.
Come inside,
Dirty and unclean,
So that I can wash your feet,"
Says Jesus.

"Try and keep them clean,
But if you can't,
I'm here to wash them.

But when I'm not here anymore,
I ask that you show
The ones with dirty feet
What it looks like to know me,"

Says resurrected Jesus.

the secret place

Jesus wept.

Why did He weep?

Well, because His friend died.

But did He weep
Because they thought
He let them down?

If that is so,
Did it foreshadow the cross?

That if He didn't go,
He would be letting us down?

I can't help but image
The thought occurring
In the garden,
When He asked for another way.

Fully human in emotion,
But fully God in power.

This time He wouldn't
Be raising another body,
But instead
Be raising *His* own.

In church,

My neck gets tired
Of watching the pastor.

My legs get tired
Of standing up.

My thoughts go elsewhere.
Questioning when service will end.

Comfortable Christianity.

The holes in His hand,
The wound in His side,
The loss of His life on the earth

He created.

Yet, not a word of complaint.

In the darkest hour,
While He was spit on,
His integrity was questioned,
The created was crucifying the Creator.

He didn't complain,
He didn't scream,
He forgave.

In the last hours,
He didn't fight against the world,
He fought for the soul of another.

He saved a soul bound for hell,
The criminal on the cross,

Is now a *child*.

Jesus grew up in a church
That He knew would kill Him.

The same people,
Taken out of slavery

By Him,

Would be the ones to

Put Him,

In chains.

the secret place

Do the holes remain?
Do the scars show the true pain?

We use the cross
As a symbol
Because using another
Would be too real.

Crosses aren't used anymore,
So it makes it more comfortable
To wear around.

If you put on the cross,
Imagine what it was like
To be on it.

Not just what it was like
To spectate it.

The lives lost,
The dedication of our
Brothers and sisters.

The Word is essential,
And they knew it.

While their letters
Were burned,
And Christ followers
Were killed,

The texts remained.

The Bible is not just
To grow your faith,

It's also to remember
The faith of generations.

Fearfully and wonderfully,
So why be someone else?

In reality, you can't,
Down to your DNA,
You can't be anyone else
But yourself.

"I hate how I look."

You're wonderfully made.

When you realize your worth,
You only give yourself the best.

"I'm not like anyone else."

"Exactly, now go tell the others,"
Says Jesus.

You are so special.

The world is lost.

The saved look at the world
With anguish and solemn.

I wish they knew
That it's not just
Sitting in a pew.

It's not a
This or that game.

It's happiness or hurt.

You don't want it
After you know Jesus.

I can't explain it.

It loses its luster.
The shine is gone.

But that doesn't mean
Sin doesn't sometimes shimmer.

Indescribable peace and rest
In the grace of Jesus.

Come home.

the secret place

Jesus slept during the storm.

If it doesn't scare Him,
Why should it you?

Storms are temporary,
And Jesus knew this.

He was just waiting
To see if you knew too.

If you preserve the storm,
The rainbow will come.

Rain is essential for growth.

I strive for belonging.

My love for the world
Is strong.

No matter what the goal,
It's never enough.

You say I'm enough,
Yet I don't believe.
I wish I felt that.

I guess I'll chase the wind
Until my legs grow weak.

I'll sit down by a tree
To catch my breath.

And as I get up,
I finally notice *Your* presence
And see the wood

That constructed the cross.

the secret place

My questions grow long,
And my knowledge grows large.

No matter how much I study,
Nothing explains the grace.

How and whys are great,
And wisdom is a gift.

But nothing can explain *You*,
The creator killed by the created.

A sinless man
For the sinners.

I wish I knew.

I would like to say
That I would have stayed

But I would have run,
Just as I do today.

Even knowing who you are
And what the outcome is.

Judas wanted a material kingdom,
I'm Judas.

Peter lied about knowing you,
I'm Peter.

Thomas said "show me the evidence,"
I'm Thomas.

So why die for me?

I don't know.

But I'm so glad

You did.

the secret place

For thirty years,
His secret remained.

But you believe that God
Is slow to answer you?

If Jesus waited,
Why can't you?

You may not be ready,
Or the time isn't right.

But one thing remains true,
Waiting is better than rushing.

Waiting grows the Spirit,
While rushing claims to know the Spirit
More than

The Spirit itself.

You turned down the temptations,
And the enemy tried hard.

We laugh at his attempt
Because *You* knew the future.

But don't we?

I give in constantly,
And I know my future.

Never let your pride
Silence your Spirit,

Because when it does,
Your complacent heart
Begins to wonder.

If the world can satisfy
More than

The Blood.

the secret place

Ending your life
Breaks my heart.

A life so special
And full of love.

Darkness overtakes one,
Convincing them that an ending
Is the only way.

I disagree.

I hate when things end.
Some of the middle is messy,
But do you remember the start?

So fresh and clean.
Maybe that's what you need.

I know just the One.

Would you let me plant

The seed?

Light should be bright,
So why aren't you shinning?

Are you scared of what
Darkness has to say?

Or is your light
Not as perfect as theirs?

Both a heavy duty
And simple flashlight
Shine a light.

They differ in purpose,
But that doesn't diminish
The need for either.

They are just meant
For certain situations.

So shine your light
Where it's the brightest,
Over the darkness it's
Faced against.

the secret place

"I spent all day working,
Getting things in order.

I did a lot of planning,
And really want it to be special.

Your going to love it,
It's all designed perfectly."

Sound familiar?

You expect someone
To appreciate the work
You've done.

So, why disagree
When God said this

About you.

Habakkuk 2

Overlaid in silver and gold,
But lifeless inside.

Instagram,
Snapchat,
Facebook.

Our lives are overlaid
With happiness and joy,

But that's what they see.

When did it become common
To sell a lie to others?

Your life is not silver and gold.

Your instagram may be,
But on the inside,
You are scared
Of what they would think
If they knew.

Jesus knows,
And He doesn't
Want you to hide.

He wants you
to be *Healed.*

Habakkuk 3

Even though the fig tree
Has no blossoms.

Your life has become stagnant.
Your'e waiting for something,
And it doesn't seem to be coming.

But stay joyful
And rejoice in *the Lord.*

Your time may never come,
And that's ok.

You are unique,
And so is your path.

God doesn't always give handouts,
So maybe you need to take the step,

Similar to the one
Of *receiving salvation.*

Matthew 18

Your debt is high,
And it's closing in.

But someone wants to pay it,
Someone who knows you,
Despite what you think

Of Him.

If you accept this forgiveness
Of extreme debt,

Their little debt must also be forgiven,
No matter if they deserve it.

So forgive and be forgiven,

Or collect debt and be

Eternally bankrupt.

Judas, despite watching Jesus,
Never recognized Him as Lord.

He always just called Him teacher,
Even after the miracles.

What do you call Him?

Teacher of moral standard
Or
Risen Messiah of moral creation?

Each one is culturally acceptable,
But only one is

Eternally acceptable.

I love being loved,
But it seems to come
Only when I have something to give.

When I don't,
I feel unworthy.

Like a lamp
That emits no light.

Maybe I'm plugged into
A dull outlet,

Or maybe I'm not finding love
In the one that created it.

How can I be loved
If I haven't known it?

If you feel unloved,
Look to Him,
And let your heart

Overflow.

If you need help,
Please reach out.

We need you here.

Asking for help
is not weak,
It's strong.

Even Jesus was aided in
Carrying the cross.

You're not a statistic,
You're a child.

A bandaid on wet skin,

It will help,
But for how long?

"I need it to get better."

But shouldn't you dry off
Before applying it?

If you hastily put it on,
The treatment will never stick.

Yet, we still do it.

That sin will never be plentiful
And heal your wound.

So wait out the pain,
Because once that bandaid
Is put on correctly,

It hurts you to take it off.

Spiritual growth.

The elders,

My heart yearns for the day
I have to say goodbye.

Im not sure I can
Handle it.

You loved me before
You saw me,

And I will love you after
I can see you.

A dreadful world.

I will see you again
Because you taught me how.

Our Lord will keep us close
When it feels that we are far.

The day you leave
Is the day I will need you most.

But I will lean on

The Holy Ghost.

I feel unique,
Like no one truly understands.

Im just different,
And that's ok.

But it is never ok
To mock someone
That's different from you.

What's the point?

Insecurity is the root,
And it must be replaced.

Because you were handcrafted,
And so were they.

When you find peace,
You can't help but share it.

So do you have it,
Or is there something
Still holding you back?

Sin has no home
In the temple,

And you are

The Temple.

We're told not to ponder
The good old days.

I think I know why.

Whether it's a good memory
Or a bad memory,

It makes us sad
That it has either
Passed or happened.

If we look back,
We're blind to the future,

And there is so much more
That Jesus has for you
In the coming days.

So be on the lookout!

Because I didn't know
I could write,

But here I am!

Let Jesus lead your path
With clear vision for

The future.

The spear was unnecessary,
But it is mighty important.

Jesus was dead.
His spirit was given up.

But they had to be certain,
Because this performance,
Could not be discredited.

They had to show that He
Was lying the whole time.

"If He was God
Why not come down?"
They said.

Oh how close-minded they were,
They didn't understand the process.

The spear was a conclusion
To their operation.

Too bad Jesus
Wrote the story,

And they had just finished

The introduction.

Your life didn't change
Because you prayed a prayer.

Your life changed
Because you finally understood

That you would never do
What Jesus claims He did.

But it's not just
a claim to you;

It's truth.

Get past the unworthy feeling.

The feeling is not wrong.
It's incredibly right.

You are unworthy
Of grace,

It's not a trap,
It's a fact.

But you have been
Set free,

Or at least I think
You have.

Maybe you're fighting guilt,
Or maybe you're fighting

Pride,

Because you could never
Do this alone
Or on your own.

I could never represent you,
Because if I did,
No one would follow you.

My words and actions
Continuously fall short.

I call myself a
Christ Follower,

But I seem to drift
From that path.

Good thing they'll follow Him
And not me, right?

When you get close,
You realize that the church
Is constructed of sinners.

But that's what
Makes it special.

You live free in Him,
Because you can never
Be Him.

But make sure
To let your fruit bear,
So you can share.

People inspire me,

More specifically,
My brothers and sisters.

Their faith inspires me
To be better.

That's growth.

A fruitful example of Jesus
To inspire my faith,

Not a rule book
To weigh me down.

I know how bad I am,
No need for further explaining.

But a empowering word
Grows the seed
Planted inside of me.

So encourage someone today,
Let them know their progress,

Because Jesus also sees it.

Sometimes you lose,
And that stinks.

But Jesus didn't fight back,
So why are you?

If you are convinced
Heaven is paradise,

Why argue with someone
About its validity?

Maybe you don't fully believe,
Or maybe you just want to be right.

But Jesus didn't die and rise
So you could win an argument.

He did it to show you
What it looks like to lose
In the present.

The only difference is,
Your body won't rise on earth.

Your soul will rise

To Heaven.

Lamentations

Where are you, God?
Do you not see us suffering?

Beautiful Jerusalem longs
For your intercession,

But you are unseen to us.

Only do they call
When sin catches them.

I don't enjoy hurting them
Or causing sorrow,
But *I* can't give you a pass.

You must be accountable,
Or you will never learn.

See how much it hurts
To stray into sin
And away from *Me*.

If sin satisfied,
It would have been
Apart of the original design.

How can He righteously judge
If He saves here, but not there?

I love getting
The last laugh.

I love firing back
After an insult is given.

But I shouldn't.
Jesus didn't.

He silently waited
And endured the names.

Because He didn't have
To speak.

His future actions
Would be so powerful,

Not even they
Could utter another word.

So let your actions
Speak for you
Instead of the

Deceitful tongue.

Jesus went to the
Desert to pray.

But maybe He went
To remember how
It all started.

From dust came man.

Sand isn't exactly dust,
But it's similar.

And maybe now,
because of our sin,

We looked more like sand
Than the original dust,

Completely different
In design and purpose.

Or maybe He just
Had to get away.

Anyway.

Sometimes I forget
That I'm reading about *You*.

I skim through
Like it's just a story.

But if I really believe
This to be true,

How could I not
pick it up daily?

Maybe this is why you don't.

You see reading
As a chore,

Instead of seeing it as
Growing with the one
You follow.

An interesting thought
That if true,
Needs to become real

To you.

I always thought
I wanted more,

But the more I have,
The less it means.

That night,
When all I had was *You,*

Was the night
I had gained the most.

Now when I experience
The many blessings from *You,*
I can't help but long for more.

Help my eyes and my soul
Focus on the little things,

Finding peace there,
Instead of nowhere.

The prodigal didn't lack blessing,
He lacked understanding.

God has blessings
For you,

But if you
Rush the plan,

You experience something
That was supposed to come later.

You may not
Want to wait,

I understand that,

But your reverence
Will pay off,
And the inheritance
Will be yours.

Remember that no matter
How good the feast tasted
When he returned,

The pig slop
Still lingered,

And the inheritance
Was still gone.

"We have to go see Jesus
He's a miraculous healer,"
They said.

I can't imagine
The distance they traveled.

They didn't have cars
Or efficient transportation,

But they would travel
Just to see Him
And be healed.

You experience
Chronic pain,
Depression,
Guilt,
Jealousy,
Physical ailments,

And won't go
To the church
Down the block.

The Spirit never changes,

It's a matter of
If you want to.

the secret place

Im the older brother,
As much as that pains me.

I do get frustrated
When it seems unfair.

How do I celebrate someone
Who knowingly disobeyed?

He spent your money.
You'll never see it again!

"But, he's back."

Since you know *The Word,*
You know that materials fade.

But *my grace* is here to stay.

I see your reverence,
But your brother
Has returned.

We must celebrate
And show him love,

So he will never
Want to leave

Again.

I battle sin,

The things it promises
Are so sweet.

How can it be so sour?

The wine given
Before your death
Symbolizes more than prophecy.

It shows how my soul feels
When sin has won.

My knees,
Mean I really messed up.

But what about those
Little sins?

Does just a simple
"Forgive me," do?

I wonder who
Gave sin hierarchy.

Probably ones that
Didn't kill or cheat,
But just lied sometimes.

Sin causes a fracture,
And if I'm not careful,
A break is imminent.

Back to my knees I go,
Even though I claimed
I wouldn't stoop that low,

Again.

I sit here
In my puddle of tears.

Wondering how the past
Is so far gone.

I wish I could go back
And enjoy it.

Everything is different,
Everyone is older,

But you are the same.

When all else
Seems wrecked
Or ever-changing,

I have *You.*

Time slips through my hands
And I can't stop it.

Everyday is a blessing,
And I need to know that.

Your hands hold my future
And hold my life.

You endured the nails
So I could live.

Yet, even with the holes,
Nothing slips through.

You hold us all,
Just as the nail held

Your body.

Do *you* look back
Like we do?

Pondering on our memories
Like a human?

Peeking back
To the night of salvation,
And wondering where
The time has gone?

Does it make *you* sad
To see the world move,

Or do *you* long
For the day

In which we come
And meet *you*?

I may not have

The perfect body,
The perfect attitude,
The perfect life,
The perfect finances,
The perfect family,
The perfect grades,
The perfect clothes,
The perfect relationships.

But I do have

The perfect savior.

Help my fruit bear.

As soon as
I see the buds

I severe my limbs
With sin.

How do I move forward?

Luckily, fruits have seeds
That grow when they fall.

So, even in my sin
Grace will revitalize my walk.

My buds will now grow.

Will I see them sprout
Or will I fall again?

Either way, I know the
Cultivating process

And it's my choice
To see the harvest.

the secret place

God, thank you
For everything you do.

Help me to
Grow in you.

Im tired of
Being stagnant.

Help my heart
To do the right thing,

Because if I truly
Want to be better

A daily sacrifice is needed.

But if I want to
Remain the same,

I'll see you Sunday morning.

You have a choice,
Life is full of them.

How will you use yours?

Are you proud
Of what you're doing?

Are you regretting
What you say?

Are you happy
With the path that you're on?

Are you feeding yourself
World or *Word?*

You have a choice everyday,

To pick up your cross
Or provide the cross.

What will it be?

"My soul is crushed with grief,
To the point of death,
Stay and keep watch with me,"
Says Jesus.

James and John follow,
But fall asleep,
While Jesus is in anguish.

Are you asleep while
One is in anguish,
Or do you stay up
And experience it together?

Jesus didn't need them,
His throne was safe,

But even through their sleep,
When they didn't care,

He suffered.

Are you in anguish
For the sanctification of others,

Or are you content
For just yours?

"Let me see the holes
In your hands,
Then I will believe,"
Says Thomas.

"Didn't you see the healings
Performed by these hands,
And the washing of feet
By these hands?

You have seen me
Do incredible wonders,
But are only fixated on me
At my lowest point.

What makes you think
A hole would show you
The proof that *I AM*
Who I say *I AM*?

Great are those who
Believe without seeing,
Yet you only believe
By seeing my hands.

If this is the case
For what's to come,
I pray the church shows
My love through their hands,

By building their light so tall,
The world can't help but notice"
Says resurrected Jesus.

The Spirit,
That raised His body,
Is inside of you.

Mustard seed faith
Is all that's required.

But you can't even
Muster that much.

Jesus's faith was agonizing,
But to see it through,
He knew what He had to do.

The door is open.

Will you close it,
Or will you live to
See the day,
Where the tomb stone

Is rolled away.

Jesus was not released
During His trial;

Instead, the people
Chose to release
A convicted murderer.

"How could they be so ignorant?"
We say.

You know the way to peace,
Yet you find comfort in
Releasing sin back into your life.

Doesn't sound
So farfetched now, does it?

Quick to judge,
But slow to see
The sin in me.

You have to find
Peace eternally,
Before you can find it

Internally.

My heart yearns for your creative mind to capture these poems. I am so grateful that you entrusted me with teaching these stories to you. I long for you to get closer to Jesus, not because of what I say, but because you desire to. I hope this book is a light in your walk and a lamp for some of your unanswered questions. You are so loved, unique, and important. I want you to realize that Jesus is not a far-off figure in history but a present savior in everyday life.
I can't thank you enough.

Made in the USA
Las Vegas, NV
28 November 2024